Vanished!

Written by Susan Griffiths

Contents Page

Chapter 1. *Extinction Is Forever!* 4

Chapter 2. *The Mighty Mammoth* 6

Chapter 3. *Dead As A Dodo* 10

Chapter 4. *Passenger Pigeons* 14

Chapter 5. *Treasured Takahe* 18

Chapter 6. *Tiger Trauma* 22

Photo Feature: *The Changing Role Of Zoos* 26

Chapter 7. *A Change Of Attitude* 28

Chart: *An Extinction Timeline* 30

Index And Bookweb Links 32

Glossary Inside Back Cover

Rigby

Chapter Snapshots

1. Extinction Is Forever! Page 4

What causes some animals to become extinct? Imagine you are a biological detective—collect clues and facts and decide who is the prime suspect in the following cases!

2. The Mighty Mammoth Page 6

Mammoths belonged to the same animal group as elephants. They could be about 15 feet tall! If they were so huge, why did they become extinct?

3. Dead As A Dodo Page 10

When dodos came into contact with people, they began to disappear from the planet. People then introduced other animals into the dodo's environment! Their fate was sealed.

"... in recent times, contributed to many

4. Passenger Pigeons Page 14

Passenger pigeons were one of the most common birds in North America. They could live for up to twenty-five years. In less than fifty years, people managed to wipe them out completely!

5. Treasured Takahe Page 18

Up until 1948, the New Zealand takahe was thought to be extinct. Scientists hope that, with careful breeding programs, the takahe can return to its natural habitat. People are finally learning to take care of *all* the animals that share our environment.

6. Tiger Trauma Page 22

The Tasmanian tiger was a large dog-like marsupial. Early settlers in Australia were afraid that it would kill their sheep and cattle, so they decided to kill it first.

7. A Change Of Attitude Page 28

Incredibly, a Tasmanian tiger was found perfectly preserved in a jar. With current cloning and genetic technology, it may be possible for people to bring back to life what they had destroyed.

one group of prime suspects
animals becoming extinct."

The Mammoth

1. Extinction Is Forever!

The Dodo

When a species of animal no longer exists, we say that it is extinct. Ever since life first appeared on our planet billions of years ago, many kinds of animals have lived and then vanished. They have become extinct. Here are some animals who met this fate, and some who are in danger today.

The Passenger Pigeon

The Takahe

The Tasmanian Tiger

Imagine you are a biological detective!

What Is Biology?

Biology is the study of living things. The word comes from two ancient Greek words: *bios*, which means *life* and *logos*, which means *to study*.

What caused the mammoth, the dodo, and the passenger pigeon to become extinct? Your job is to find out!

As a biological detective, you will read about the animal victim, the scene of the crime and the *motive*—or reason—for the crime. Then you will write about what has happened and who might be the prime suspects.

Detective Work

A detective is someone who collects clues and facts about a crime. Using information they gather, detectives must then decide who they think did the crime. That person is called the "prime suspect."

You will find that, in recent times, *one* group of prime suspects has contributed to the extinction of *many* animals. That group of prime suspects is: **Us!**

2. The Mighty Mammoth

EXTINCTION INVESTIGATION FILE

Victims: .... Mammoths.

Place Victims Found: North America, Asia, Russia, and other parts of Europe.

Time Of Extinction: .... 10,000 years ago.

Prime Suspects: .... Human beings.

Method: .... Arrows and spears.

Clues: .... Bones, tusks, fur, bodies, and cave paintings.

DESCRIPTION OF VICTIM:

Mammoths belonged to the same animal family as elephants. Today there are only two types of elephants—the African elephant and the smaller Indian elephant.

Elephant	African Elephant.	Indian Elephant.
Weight	15,000 lbs.	11,000 lbs.
Length	25 ft.	21 ft.
Ears	Large and round.	Small and triangular.
Habitat	Africa.	Southeast Asia.

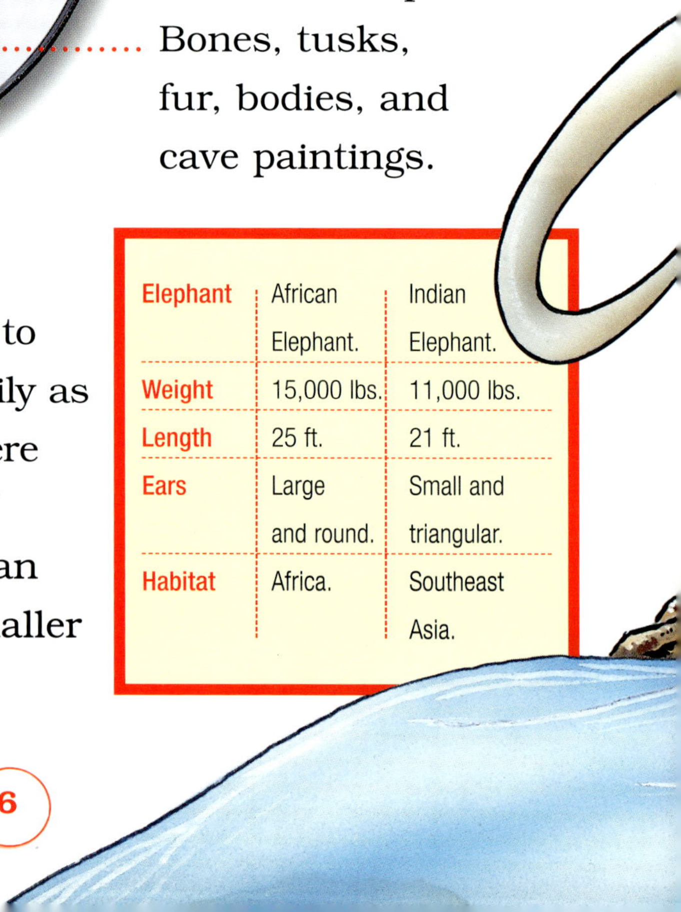

A Very Large Elephant

A long time ago, there were at least 160 different types of animals that belonged to the elephant family. All but two have vanished from the Earth.

Scientists have found bones, tusks, fur, and body parts from seven different types of mammoths. The largest type of mammoth stood about 15 feet high, and their tusks could be as long as 16 feet.

SCENE OF THE CRIME:

Mammoths lived in North America, Asia, Siberia, and other parts of Europe. About 15,000 years ago in Europe, people who lived in caves painted pictures of mammoths. In these pictures, we see people hunting mammoths. This provides us with a clue about why they became extinct.

Frozen Mammoths!

Unlike many animals that became extinct thousands of years ago, we know quite a lot about mammoths.

Usually when an animal becomes extinct, only its bones and fossils are left for us to study. The softer parts of the animal, like its muscles, hair, and internal organs, are eaten by other animals or they decay.

But many mammoths lived in such cold parts of the world as Siberia in Russia. Amazingly, whole mammoths have been discovered frozen underground in Siberia. Scientists could tell what color they were, what sort of hair they had, and what they looked like when they were alive.

MOTIVE:

Although it must have been dangerous for early people to hunt mammoths, they were very important for human survival. The meat from a mammoth would feed a group of families for a long time. People could use the hairy skins for clothing and for shelter. And in some cold places, the bones of the mammoth were used to build tents and huts. Thousands of mammoth bones have been discovered in areas where people hunted them for many years.

WHAT HAPPENED:

About 10,000 years ago, mammoths became extinct. Scientists today think that people hunting too many mammoths, together with a change in the climate from warm to very, very cold, caused the mammoths to become extinct.

VERDICT ON PRIME SUSPECT:

People are partly guilty!

GUILTY!

3. Dead As A Dodo

EXTINCTION INVESTIGATION FILE

Victims:.. Dodos.
Place Victims Found:......... Mauritius.
Time Of Extinction:.......... 1680.
Prime Suspects:................... Human beings.
Method:.. Clubs, traps, and guns.
Clues:.. Paintings, feathers, preserved bodies in museums.

DESCRIPTION OF VICTIM:

The dodo was a type of pigeon, about the size of a turkey. Today, if someone calls a person a "dodo," they usually mean that the other person is not very smart. This describes how people thought of these large, flightless birds. But people weren't very smart about the way they treated dodos all those years ago!

Flightless Birds

Long ago, on many islands, there were no predators to hunt and eat birds. The birds did not need to fly and so gradually lost this skill. Birds such as kiwis and moas adapted well to life on the ground. But, like the dodo, they faced serious danger with the arrival of human beings.

SCENE OF THE CRIME:

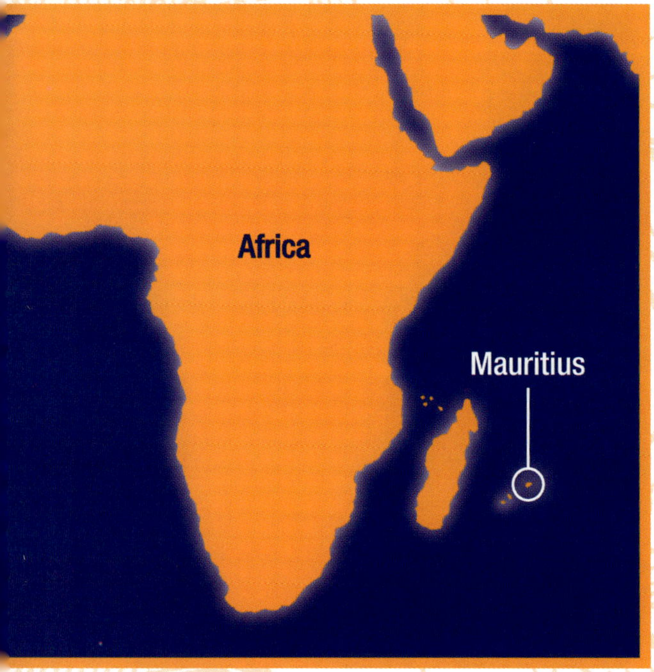

The dodo lived on an island called Mauritius near the east coast of Africa. Dodos had lived there for millions of years, but when they came into contact with people, they quickly became extinct. Before people arrived on Mauritius, there were no animals that hunted the dodo, so it did not need to fly. Instead, it could run only very slowly.

MOTIVE:

When sailors from Europe began to visit Mauritius around the year 1500, they hunted large numbers of the dodo for fresh meat. Sailors who visited the island thought the dodo was a stupid bird because it was so easy to catch and kill. It was such easy prey, in fact, that in a very short time, every single dodo would be killed.

Did You Know?

"Dodo" comes from the Portuguese word for "stupid!"

WHAT HAPPENED:

About a hundred years later, people started to settle on Mauritius, and more and more dodos were hunted and killed. People also brought other animals, such as dogs, with them. These new animals also hunted the dodo.

By the year 1680, the dodo was extinct. In less than 200 years, people had made the dodo vanish forever.

VERDICT ON PRIME SUSPECT:

People are guilty!

Introduced Animals

Wherever humans traveled, they brought animals with them. Some animals, like cats and dogs, they brought deliberately. Others, like rats and mice, hid in ships and escaped when the ships arrived at new lands.

Animals that have been brought to an area by people are called "introduced" animals. They can harm native animals by hunting and killing them or by eating their eggs or food.

GUILTY!

4. Passenger Pigeons

EXTINCTION INVESTIGATION FILE

Victims:.. Passenger Pigeons.
Place Victims Found:......... North America.
Time Of Extinction:.......... 1914.
Prime Suspects:.................. Human beings.
Method:.. Guns.
Clues:.. Paintings, eye-witness accounts, preserved birds in museums.

DESCRIPTION OF VICTIM:

The passenger pigeon was about the size of the common pigeon that lives in many parts of the world today. It was a gentle, harmless bird that ate seeds and nuts. It could live for up to twenty-five years—until people started to kill them in huge numbers.

SCENE OF THE CRIME:

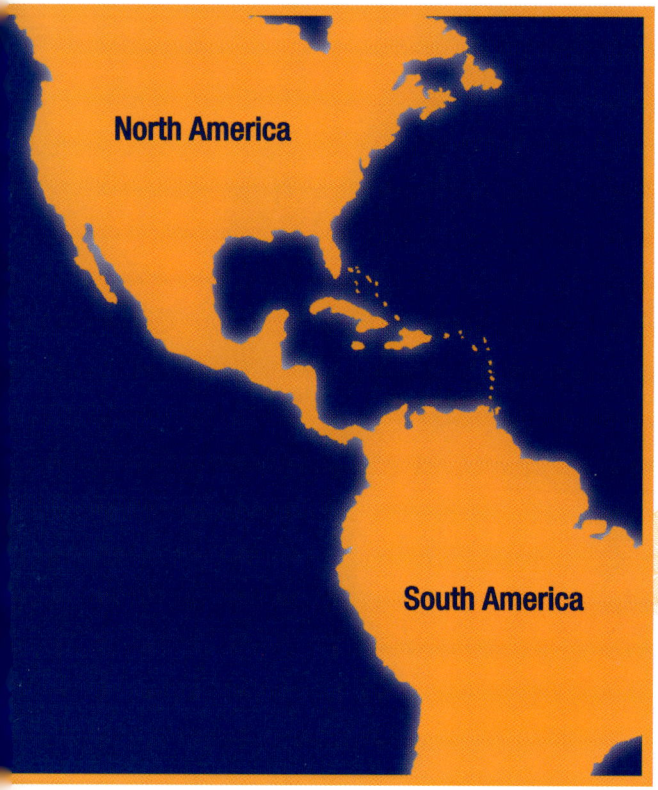

The extinction of the passenger pigeon was even more incredible than the extinction of the dodo. Up until a hundred and fifty years ago, passenger pigeons were one of the most *common* birds in North America. There were so many passenger pigeons that flocks of over a billion birds, hundreds of miles long, could be seen flying across the country. Yet, in fifty years, people had killed so many of them that they became extinct.

MOTIVE:

The passenger pigeons became extinct because they were so useful to people. Because there were so many of them, they were the cheapest kind of meat that people could buy. Every day, in almost every city in North America, thousands of pigeons were killed for food. Their insides were used for medicines and their feathers were used for pillows and blankets. People also hunted huge numbers of pigeons for sport.

WHAT HAPPENED:

By 1896, there were only 250,000 passenger pigeons left, in one large flock. But no one seemed to consider that, soon, they might become extinct. Hunters followed this flock and killed almost all of it.

In 1900, the last wild passenger pigeon was shot by a young boy. In 1914, the last known passenger pigeon, which was held in a zoo, died. It took people less than fifty years, to make the most common bird in North America become extinct.

Inventions And The Passenger Pigeon

As people built railways across North America, they used them to kill even more pigeons and transport them to the cities.

With the invention of the telegraph, a machine that could send messages through wires, hunters could tell each other where the huge flocks of birds were heading. The passenger pigeon was doomed.

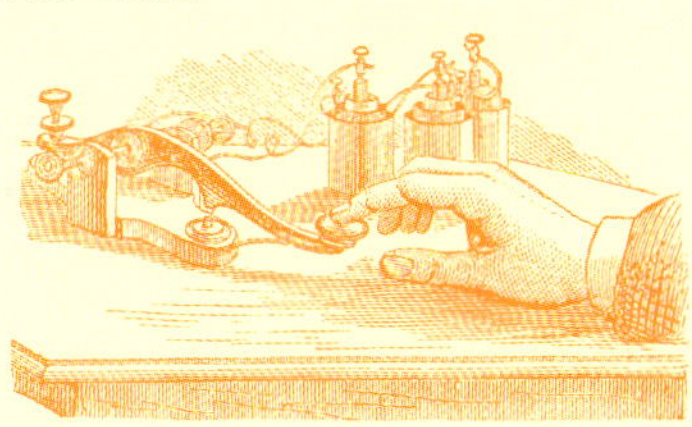

VERDICT ON PRIME SUSPECT:

People are guilty!

GUILTY!

5. Treasured Takahe

EXTINCTION INVESTIGATION FILE

Victims:.. Takahe.
Place Victims Found:........ New Zealand.
Time Of Extinction:.......... 1880.
Prime Suspects:................. Human beings.
Method:.............................. Dogs, cats, rats, deer.
Clues:................................. Bones, feathers, paintings, preserved birds in museums.

CASE REOPENED 1948: BIRDS FOUND ALIVE AND WELL!

DESCRIPTION OF VICTIM:

Before people lived in New Zealand, there were many types of unique and unusual birds that lived in the forests. The takahe was one such bird. A large flightless bird, the takahe had beautiful green-blue feathers and ate plants and insects from the forest floor.

SCENE OF THE CRIME:

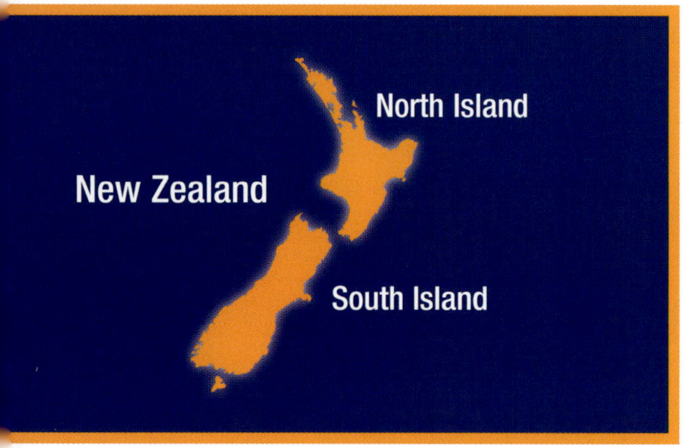

Before people arrived in New Zealand more than a thousand years ago, the takahe was widespread throughout the islands of New Zealand. With the arrival of people, the numbers of takahe rapidly started to decline.

MOTIVE:

People burned down many of the forests where the takahe lived. They also brought with them rats, cats, dogs, and deer. These animals hunted the takahe, ate their eggs, or ate their food. Although human beings did not deliberately hurt the takahe, their actions caused them to become very rare, especially during the 1800s. By the end of the 1800s, the takahe was thought to be extinct.

WHAT HAPPENED:

Then, in 1948, an amazing discovery was made. Deep in a rugged, unexplored area of the South Island of New Zealand, a small group of takahe were discovered alive.

The government knew that something had to be done to protect this rare bird species. For the first time, they decided to try a "captive breeding" program.

Takahe chicks are fed by puppets in the captive breeding program.

A Success Story

Eggs from the wild takahe were taken to a farm in the North Island of New Zealand and ordinary hens were used to hatch them. The young takahe were brought up in captivity and produced more eggs, which were also carefully hatched.

Eventually, scientists learned enough about the takahe to continue their captive breeding program with much success. They hope that enough takahe will be born in captivity to allow some birds to go back into the wild.

BEHAVING BETTER!

At last, after ten thousand years of behavior that caused animals to become extinct, human beings have finally started working to find ways of saving animals from extinction.

VERDICT ON PRIME SUSPECT:

People trying to behave better, AT LAST!

6. Tiger Trauma

EXTINCTION INVESTIGATION FILE

Victims:.. Tasmanian Tiger.
Place Victims Found:.......... Australia.
Time Of Extinction:............ 1933.
Prime Suspects:.................... Human beings.
Method:................................... Guns.
Clues:...................................... Photographs, films, paintings, eye-witness descriptions, preserved animals in museums.

DESCRIPTION OF VICTIM:

Whenever people find a new place to live, they have an effect on the animals that live there. For millions of years, Australia has been home to many types of unique and unusual animals called marsupials.

Kangaroos are marsupials.

Tiger Or Wolf?

Marsupials are unique because they keep their babies in pouches.

The Tasmanian tiger, or thylacine, was a large dog-like marsupial with strong jaws and a long tail.

Because the thylacine reminded many settlers of the wolves common in Europe and North America, it was sometimes called the Tasmanian wolf.

SCENE OF THE CRIME:

The Tasmanian tiger once lived all over Australia. Scientists think that it became extinct on the mainland of Australia because of the introduction of the dingo, or wild dog, by early Aboriginal people. By the time that Europeans arrived in Australia during the 1800s, the Tasmanian tiger had already vanished from the mainland. It only survived on the island of Tasmania, where there were no dingoes.

Thylacinus cynocephalus

The scientific name for the Tasmanian tiger is *Thylacinus cynocephalus*, which means "pouched dog with a wolf head." This is a very good description of how the Tasmanian tiger looked. The Tasmanian tiger was a nocturnal animal that hunted kangaroos, wallabies, and small birds.

MOTIVE:

When Europeans began farming in Tasmania, they were worried that the Tasmanian tiger was going to kill and eat their sheep and cattle. In 1888, the government of Tasmania offered a reward for every Tasmanian tiger that was killed. Over the next twenty years, thousands of the animals were killed.

WHAT HAPPENED:

By the 1930s, hunting and dog diseases introduced by the settlers' dogs made the Tasmanian tiger very rare. The last one killed in the wild was shot in 1930. The last one ever caught was captured in 1933 and kept in a Tasmanian zoo, where it soon died.

Although thylacines are thought to have been extinct since 1933, some people claim to have seen or heard Tasmanian tigers recently. In 1966, the Tasmanian government set aside an area of the island as a reserve for the animal, hoping that it still existed.

VERDICT ON PRIME SUSPECT:

People are guilty!

GUILTY!

The last Tasmanian tiger was kept in a zoo, where it soon died.

The Changing Role Of Zoos

For thousands of years, people have kept animals in zoos. The Roman emperor Nero kept a tiger named Phoebe in his private zoo. The emperor Charlemagne, who ruled much of Europe 1,200 years ago, also had a large zoo. His favorite animal was an elephant called Abul Aba!

Until about fifty years ago, most zoos kept animals mostly as entertainment for their visitors. Animals were often kept in crowded, unnatural conditions.

Today's zoos are very different places. They have two vital roles: to educate their visitors about the importance of conservation, and to carefully breed endangered species so they do not become extinct. Zoos are committed to saving the 2,000 endangered animal species at risk of extinction, and have had much success in doing so.

7. A Change Of Attitude

In 1999, a baby Tasmanian tiger was discovered in a museum preserved in a large jar. With new technology and knowledge of biology, scientists will try to use cells from the preserved baby to grow a real-live Tasmanian tiger.

It sounds like something that might happen in the movies, but in a few years time, it may well be possible.

This perfectly preserved Tasmanian tiger may be brought back to life through cloning and genetic technology.

In recent years, people have become more aware of the effect that they have on animals and plants in their environment. They have also learned how important it is to protect and preserve as many types of animals as possible. This change in attitude has meant that many endangered species are now being carefully monitored and kept safe.

There are only about 250,000 African elephants left in the wild.

Sometimes, we are surprised when animals that we thought had become extinct turn up alive and well. Today we know that when we find a rare or endangered species, we must look after it and make sure it doesn't become extinct!

Success Story

The Arabian oryx, which looks like a long-horned antelope, was extinct in the wild in the 1970s. Only a few remained in zoos. But by 1982, enough had been bred in zoos to release some back into the wild. The work of zoos saved the oryx from certain extinction!

An Extinction Timeline

		15,000 years ago	10,000 years ago	Year 1500	Year 1600	Year 1700	Year 1800	Year 1900	Year 191
Takahe							1880 Takahe thought to be extinct.	TAKAHE EXTINCT?	
Tasmanian Tigers									
Passenger Pigeons							1896 Only 250,000 passenger pigeons alive.	1900 Last wild pigeon shot.	19 La pig die in
Dodos				1500 Sailors visit Mauritius.	1600 People settle in Mauritius.	DODOS EXTINCT!			
Mammoths			MAMMOTHS EXTINCT!						

Dates

1948
Small group of takahe discovered alive!

TAKAHE NOT EXTINCT!

Careful breeding programs may help scientists reestablish takahe in the wild.

1930
Tasmanian tigers become a rare animal.

1933
Last Tasmanian tiger dies in a zoo.

TASMANIAN TIGERS EXTINCT!

1966
Area set aside for the Tasmanian tiger in the hope that it is still alive.

1999
Tasmanian tiger found preserved in a jar.

PIGEONS EXTINCT!

Year 1920	Year 1930	Year 1940	Year 1950	Year 1960	Year 1970	Year 1980	Year 1990	Year 2000

Index

animals
- endangered 26, 29
- introduced 13

Asia 6
Australia 22, 24
captive breeding 21
cats 13, 18, 20
deer 18, 20
detective 5
dodo 4, 10–13, 30–31
dogs 13, 18, 20
elephants
- African 6, 29
- Indian 6

extinction
- causes 5, 8, 9, 13, 16, 17, 24, 25

inventions 17
kiwis 11
mammoth 4, 6–9, 30–31
- frozen 8
- hunting 8, 9
- tusks 7
- types 7

marsupials 22, 23
Mauritius 10, 12–13
mice 13
moas 11
New Zealand 11, 18, 20, 21
North America 6, 14, 16
oryx 29
passenger pigeon 4, 14–17, 30–31
rats 13, 18, 20
Russia 6, 8
takahe 4, 18–21, 30–31
Tasmanian tiger (thylacine) 4, 22–27, 28, 30–31
zoos 25, 26, 29

Bookweb Links

More Bookweb books
about extinct and endangered animals!

The Mammoth Hunters—Fiction
Time Capsule—Fiction
Jaguar Attack!—Fiction

Key To Bookweb

Fact Boxes

- ☐ Arts
- ☐ Health
- ☐ Science
- ☐ Social Studies
- ☐ Technology

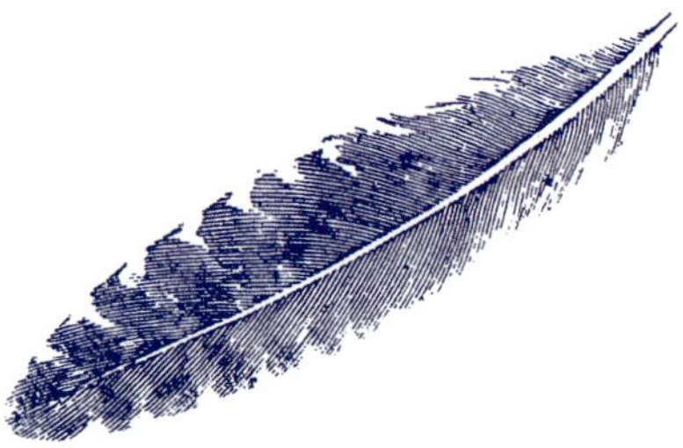